tea & biscuits

Michelle Bigaignon

BookLeaf
Publishing

India | USA | UK

Presentation by *BookLeaf Publishing*

Web: www.bookleafpub.com

E-mail: info@bookleafpub.com

ISBN: 9789357446761

First edition 2022

For my mum,

Who always encouraged me to take the first
step; here I am, starting to walk.

PREFACE

All of the emotions portrayed in these poems I have felt in my life at some point or another. The sadness, the discovery, the insecurity, the happiness, these are all me.

These poems were originally written for the twenty-somethings roaming the earth, but as I added to my collection I realised that you don't have to be in your twenties to doubt, change or question; these dealings are an occurrence throughout our lives.

So, as you flick through the pages I hope you find comfort and can safely nestle in some of my thoughts, the same way I find comfort in an afternoon tea with a side of biscuits.

All my love,

Michelle

The Beginning.

My mind is my prison,
My thoughts my escape.
I am trapped by my choices.

Let me free thoughts,
Let me sleep thoughts,
Let me be thoughts,
Set me free thoughts.

To the women in my life,

You have proven that you are strong, you have
proven that you are compassionate,
how do I prove that I fit?
You have shown me how you can endure, can be
enthralled, excited.
I can show you how I escape.
My mind is not one with my body, at all times of
the day.
It wonders, skips, leaps and then returns,
knowing little of what it's missed of my life.
I can show you how I run without moving, how I
hide whilst still being seen.
I am not a part of your world yet, even though
you are a part of mine.
I will learn to be strong, learn to laugh when it
gets hard, be excited, forget, forgive, be present.
But for now, until I know how to be like you,
I will run with my feet standing still,
I will hide in the crevasses of my mind,
Until I am ready.

21.

3

We lie in silence.
The only noise sounds when we change position,
When we breathe.
Our movements cry anger.
Our breath annoyance.
LEAVE US ALONE.
We're adults.
We're only kids.
We're lost.
We know what we're doing.
Leave us alone.
Help us.

Silence.

Can there be true silence when you are left alone with your mind?
My mind screams, it cries, it rejoices, it sings.
My mind cannot be silent.
I sink deep into my thoughts and there I find a story, a memory, colours.
My mind cannot keep still.
It runs, it leaps, it falls, I fall.
I open my eyes and realise I drifted off into a dream, sleep.
Quiet but not silent.
Motionless but not still.
I like the silence.

Who am I?

5

I feel sad.
I feel heavy.
My brain is cluttered, my thoughts unclear.
My body feels weak, I breathe slowly.
Slow.
I can't cry.
I just stare.
I feel empty.
I feel heavy.
I feel sad.

Career.

Reach for the stars,
But beware.
The stars may not be stars,
When you get up there.
They may not shine their light,
Or look quite as bright,
When you finally reach those stars.
From a distance they're ideal,
From a distance they don't reveal.
Be careful, there are things
That the bright lights conceal.
Reach for the stars
But beware.
You need to be aware.
Not everything shines once you get up there.

This is Adulthood.

7

When people said you need balance I never
knew they meant a balance between being
Selfish and Selfless.
Independent and Dependent.
Flexible and Stubborn.
I've spent my life balancing the wrong things.

Ode to Life.

8

As the seasons change and the days grow longer,
The air carries stories of summer nights.
Blossoms bloom as they should,
Some trees wish that they could,
And the sun warms your skin leaving you
radiant.
You laugh and you smile, afternoon turns to
dusk.
Today, you felt alive.
Oh, wonder and glory!
How lucky we are,
To be well and to feel so alive.

Childish.

I always have these childish dreams filled with
toys I wish I had.
Dolls with full skirts,
A mermaid that flirts,
With coloured hair that makes her look mad.

She dances and sings with her mermaid
companion,
So gentle, so elegant, so free.
Skips into my night dreams and into my
daydreams,
Stop dreaming, I think that's the key.

I'm grown up I guess,
Serious books, serious stuff.
This, is the reason I stopped reading.
The fun was all gone,
Packed up, but hold on,
Where is this new path really leading?

So, I'll read books in private,
With pictures and stories,
That makes life seem simple and carefree.
I'll listen to that small voice,
Buy pencils and markers.
I'll realise that small voice is me.

And I'll still dream of that doll with her skirt and
her smile,
That doll that I really have wanted for a while.
And that mermaid who flirts with her tail and
her hair,
And hope that one day,
I'm too childish to care.

Charlie.

Out of sight out of mind,
I guess that saying is true,
I hide the toy behind my back,
And boy, did I fool you.
Gasp, there's a surprise,
Gasp, uh oh, oh no,
Gasp, what's that, what's this?
Take my finger, let's go.
Here's a teddy,
Here's a ball,
Here's some leggo,
Take them all.
Up to your bed,
Turn off the light,
Close your eyes,
Good night.

To the children in my life,

You make life seem so simple.
You beam and squeal, carefree.
To you this world is magic.
For you, it's as good as can be.

Such small things make you giggle,
Such small things make you say,
"Wow! This is a really cool house",
"Mum, I had the best day".

To the children whom I love,
You really don't need much.
Someone you can play with,
Someone with a loving touch.

When night time comes around,
You yawn and rub your eyes.
Tomorrow more adventures,
Just waiting in the skies.

The Secret.

13

They say that adults lose their minds,
Their heads but not their hearts.
They say that adults have no time to dream, to
watch time pass.
They have their grace, their strength, their wit,
But somehow they lose their power.
The pressure of the world will always turn their
sweet to sour.
Night time stories from tales to gossip,
Garden from play to work.
But deep down in the world of souls, an adult's
dream still lurks.
Night time comes and dreams are filled with
wishes not yet come true.
Adults can dream and wish and hope and still be
adults too?

Him.

14

Your smile could move mountains,
Your happiness becomes you.
Your joy knows no limits.
The world falls into you,
A tight embrace,
A warm salute.
Electrical excitement fills our hearts.
Jubilance personified.

Dear me,

15

I write a letter with my heart and lock it with a
key,
For when I'm down, for when I doubt, a letter
addressed to 'me'.
This letter holds the secrets that I've locked
within my soul.
When I forget how great I am, or how great I'm
yet to be.

Love.

Love lifts you up.
Love embraces you.
Love calls you forth.
Face to face with Love.
Love cradles your heart.
Love unveils, conquers,
Sunshine and rain,
And all things juxtaposed.
Beginning, end,
Then, now,
You, me,
Love.

Anxiety.

17

A drumbeat pulse,
Breathe before you break.
Transfixed and terrified,
I shrink into myself.
Afraid and unaware,
Anchored by doubt,
Drowned by an overflow of thoughts.
I can't still this tremor.

Home.

I sit with you here in our house, in our home.
We skip from room to room.
There's love in the pantry, in the rugs, in the
cups; we chose them.
We put them all there.
In this house that we built, where all good things
are real,
Our hearts speak truth and sing praises.
I'm bound to you, my love, not by possessions,
but by spirit.
With you, I will forever fall.

Family.

19

Love, care, shelter.
Bestowed upon you.
A guard of honour,
A family shield.
Nestle tightly,
Fly cautiously,
Land proudly,
The wind beneath your wings.

Diary.

20

I write my feelings to understand my feelings.
To read my feelings, I truly see my feelings.
I can hear my feelings and act upon my feelings.
To write my feelings,
Sets me free.

Can I?

21

Doubt is very easy to access.
Self-loathing unhinged.
More sought after than the iridescent confidence
that no one seems to truly possess.
Doubt holds hands with procrastination.
Foes dressed as friends.

Breathe.

22

I live within my mind instead of living in the
world.
Overthink, overdo, too controlled, out of control.

Gain perspective and forget what it was like
before you found it, before you held it, before
you tamed it.

It's really not that bad, the world, once you live
outside yourself.
Less to control, yet more controlled.

Peace at last.